Listen—God is Speaking

Gaining A New Respect for The Word of God

Joe McKeever

Parson's Porch Books

www.parsonsporchbooks.com

Listen—God is Speaking

ISBN: Softcover 978-1-951472-13-9

Copyright © 2019 by Joe McKeever

All rights reserved. No part of this book may be reproduced or transmitted in any form or by any means, electronic or mechanical, including photocopying, recording, or by any information storage and retrieval system, without permission in writing from the publisher.

Listen—God is Speaking

Dedication

To my big brother Ronnie.

Rev. Ronald J. McKeever, preacher of God's infallible, inerrant Word for nearly 60 years, pastor of some outstanding churches. Through it all, battling diabetes since you were in your mid-20s. You are a champion and I'm honored to be on the same team as you.

INTRODUCTION

When I was eight years old, my coal miner Dad told me, "Son, come on and go with me." We walked down off that West Virginia mountain to the hollow where the train tracks led to nearby Sophia, WV a mile away. We walked in silence and I had no idea what was going on.

I was the third of four boys and the fourth of six children. My Dad was a good man with some rough edges. His language could peel the paint off the water tower and the whippings he put on his children were legendary. Dad never went to church, although Mom had all six children there every Sunday without fail. (God blessed her faithfulness: two of the boys became preachers.)

What happened that day was a puzzle.

When we arrived at Sophia, we walked into a "Five and Dime" store. Dad said to the sales lady, "Where are your Bibles?" She directed us to a display off to one side.

All the Bibles, maybe a dozen or fifteen, were black, KJV, and nearly identical.

Dad said, "Pick you one out."

I was so stunned, I said, "Sir?"

"Pick you out a Bible."

I did. I chose one with a zipper lining. It cost $2.98 and was the prettiest thing I'd ever seen.

Dad never explained why he did that--bought a Bible for me and not for any of the others--and I never asked.

I read that Bible every night for years. When I was 13, our house burned with everything in it. But the lovely little Bible had done its job.

That was the first of many Bibles God would use to speak His word to my heart.

These days, like most Christians I know, I own a shelf full of Bibles. I have my Grandma Bessie McKeever's Bible which she marked up and filled with mementos. I have the Bible my roommate Joel Davis gave me on my 1962 ordination. And, yes, I have a black zippered Bible, bought not long ago mostly for nostalgia, but which I love and preach from.

I have a lifelong love affair with the Word of God.

It has been my constant companion, and an unfailing guide. It has instructed me when I was not sure where to go, called me back when I was taking a wrong path, and blessed me with its assurances and comforts more times than I can remember.

You hold in your hands a book about God's book.

That's what this is.

Don't look for an order or sequence to the chapters. It's a collection of things from my mind and heart in praise of God's Word over recent years. We lifted them straight from my website (www.joemckeever.com) and tried to fine-tune them, taking out the dated stuff, deleting typos, leaving the best stuff (in my humble opinion, as the saying goes).

It bothers me to see people falling for the two great lies out of hell concerning God's word:

--1) That no one can understand this Book, that it's too contradictory or complex or whatever. Not true.

--2) that "you already know this Book. You've read it all your life. It's boring." The simple fact is no one knows it all, least of all a person who would fall for such a flimsy come-on from the all-time champion liar.

Over a half century ago, I recall a conversation in which a young man was giving all the reasons he would not be accepting a friend's invitation to a Bible study. "No one believes that stuff anymore. It's full of contradictions, it's been proven to be historically inaccurate, it's all myths. No one who is intellectually honest believes that." His friend responded, "Charlie, speaking of intellectual honesty?" "Yeah?" "What do you think of someone who does a critical book review on a book he's not even read?"

I suspect most critics of Holy Scriptures have never read it for themselves with an open mind but are merely parroting someone else's gripes.

At every opportunity, we challenge people to read God's Book. To see for themselves how powerful and relevant, how alive it is. (It claims that for itself, by the way, in Hebrews 4:12.)

If *our* book helps someone turn aside and come to love *that* Book, we will be greatly pleased.

CHAPTER ONE

The One Book for Your Entire Life!

What great nation is there that has statutes and judgments as righteous as this whole law which I am setting before you today? (Deuteronomy 4:8)

A national news columnist was telling of visiting his 90-year-old mother, a retired librarian. She had always been a voracious reader.

"Son," she told him, "I've just finished reading the most fascinating book."

As she showed it to him, he smiled.

"Mother," said the son, "I distinctly remember you telling me you had read that twenty years ago. In fact, you bought me a copy. Don't you remember?"

"The way my memory is going," she said, "honestly, I could just own one book."

We smile at the idea of reading one book over and over again. Those of us who have attained, shall we say, a certain age can identify.

And yet, focusing on one book is exactly what disciples of the Lord Jesus do. We read the Holy Bible every day and plan to do so for the rest of our days. We read it to understand it, to know the Lord better, and we read it in order to know how to serve Him.

Perhaps most of all, we read the Bible for reasons unknown to us, simply to receive whatever the Lord chooses to give us that day.

We will never progress beyond this Book. It contains the revelation of the Creator of the universe for the residents of this small planet.

There is no bottom to its depth. No end to its revelation.

We never exhaust its contents, never mine all its riches. It is inexhaustible.

Late one afternoon, I rested for a couple of hours in the home of friends in McComb, Mississippi, before attending a church banquet where I was to speak. In the living room shelves contained the books of Jan Karon, John Grisham, David Baldacci, and other popular novelists. Looks like we read the same stuff, I thought. And another thought occurred…

You won't find those books in shelves at my house for one big reason: After we read them, we're through with them. We pass them on to family members or donate them to the library or a thrift store. The one thing we never do is pull out a novel to read again, to see if we missed anything the first time through. And yet...

We do this with the Holy Scriptures all the time. Every time we pass through a familiar chapter or well-known story, we find something new, something we had not seen before. It's an amazing thing.

Finding new insights in the old stories.

This is exactly what the Lord said would happen. Matthew 13:52 contains the only mention of this in Scripture and it's a keeper....

Therefore, every scribe who has become a disciple of the kingdom of heaven is like a head of a household, who brings forth out of his treasure things new and old.

It's a fascinating image: A homeowner goes into his wall safe or that chest up in the attic and counts out all the deeds, money, jewels, and other keepsakes he has owned through the years. But something strange happens. Every time he goes there, he finds something new. A pearl ring this time, a hundred-dollar bill last time, a necklace the time before.

He'd come often, wouldn't he?

Our Lord Jesus said a scribe—someone considered an expert on the Scriptures—who gets saved will now return to the Scriptures that he loves and where he has found all these precious truths and insights. As expected, he finds them there, all the riches he has loved over the years. But to his delight, every time he comes, he makes a new discovery. A new treasure he had not seen before. A valuable insight. A precious revelation.

This treasure had been there all the time, but only after being saved was the scribe able to identify it for what it is.

And so it is with God's Word, the greatest treasure of them all.

This is what happened to Saul of Tarsus after his conversion. In Galatians 1, Paul says after his Damascus Road experience, "I did not confer with flesh and blood, nor did I go up to Jerusalem to see the apostles." So, what did he do?

"I went to Arabia." For three years. (Galatians 1:17-18).

He does not say what he was doing during that time (an equal length, incidentally, to the time the apostles had spent with Jesus). But I think we know. He was searching the Scriptures, those beloved treasures he already knew from his rabbinical studies (see Acts 22:3). And he was bringing forth treasures from them, such as we see throughout all his epistles. In Romans and Galatians, in particular, we reap the benefit of Paul's time away with the Lord for a retooling of his scriptural understanding.

So--What are you finding in God's Word?

There are so many reasons for God's people studying and living in the Scriptures. Jesus called it our bread (Matthew 4:4). Job said it was more than his necessary food (Job 23:12). David called it a lamp unto his feet, a light unto his path (Psalm 119:105). Paul said it's the source of faith (Romans 10:17).

Satan uses two lies to keep us from the Word…

–to believers, the devil says, "You already know this word. You don't need to read it." He's not complimenting you, friend, but trying to mislead you. Jesus called him a liar and the father of lies. (John 8:44).

The truth is you do not know the Word. Not really. You and I may know a lot of it. We might even be a preacher or professor and have made a study of the Bible our lifelong vocation. But there is so much we do not understand. This Holy Scripture is inexhaustible, a depth with no bottom. One might study it for a lifetime and never know it all.

–to everyone else, the devil says, "No one can understand the Bible. It's contradictory, too complex, too whatever." He's wrongs again. Even a child can glean a great deal from Scriptures. Paul said from his childhood, Timothy had known the Scriptures (2 Timothy 3:15).

The Lord Jesus called Satan a liar of the first order. He should know since He has known that one, he called the serpent, a deceiver, and a liar from the beginning.

Let's get into the Word!

Encouraging God's people to get serious about reading and studying and obeying the Word of God is what this little book is all about.

Shhh. God is speaking. Are you listening?

Here is some ancient advice: *Walk prudently when you go to the house of God and draw near to listen rather than to give the sacrifice of fools, for they do not know they do evil. Do not be rash with your mouth and let not your heart utter anything hastily before God. For God is in heaven and you on earth; Therefore, let your words be few.* (Ecclesiastes 5:1-2)

We listen in order to obey Him, to please Him. After all...

--"Everyone who hears these words of Mine and *does* them is like a wise man who builds his house on a rock...." (Matthew 7:24).

--"If you know these things, blessed are you if you *do them*" (John 13:17).

--"Why call ye me 'Lord, Lord' and *do* not the things I tell you?" (Luke 6:46).

If you call yourself a sincere disciple of the Lord Jesus Christ, this Word is your daily nourishment.

If you are a longtime disciple of Christ, there is no excuse for your not knowing the Word.

It's never too late to begin.

CHAPTER TWO

There are many reasons to believe. Scripture gives us the best reason.

"Always be ready to give a defense (answer) to anyone who asks you a reason for the hope that is in you, with meekness and fear, having a good conscience...." (I Peter 3:15-16).

Knowing you believe is not enough.

Christians should be able to state why they believe.

And, it's not enough to say, as a Mormon college professor did to me once, "I know (his book) is true because it gives me a warm feeling inside."

Most of us would require more reason than that to stake our lives on a teaching or doctrine.

While doing research for an article on The Trinity, I found myself absorbed in John Ortberg's *Know Doubt*, specifically the chapter on "Why I believe." I would read a page or two and stop. I would read more and stop. I found myself wondering: How does Ortberg do this?

Listen—God is Speaking

How can any writer fill one page with so many fascinating insights?

His book is so dense, I want to mark up every sentence and memorize every paragraph.

It's a special writer who can do this to us.

John Ortberg, author of some unforgettable best-sellers such as *If You Want to Walk on the Water, You've Got to Get Out of the Boat* and *When the Game is Over, It All Goes Back in the Box,* pastors the Menlo Park Presbyterian Church in the California city of that name.

This is the paragraph that set me off: "I believe there is a God for a pile of reasons: dreams, arguments, banana cream pie, umpires, *Hotel Rwanda,* complicated telephone mailbox systems, Little Nell, the happiness pill, and one other reason, one reason that trumps every other reason and leaves them all in the dust."

Then, he takes that sentence apart and says why each of those "reasons" matters to him, and what they bring to his faith.

Reading him, I thought, "Anyone can do this. Anyone can make a similar list of reasons they believe in the existence of God and the reality of the Spirit world and the truthfulness of the Word."

So, before revealing Ortberg's "one other reason," the one that "trumps every other reason and leaves them all in the dust," I'll posit a few of my own.

I believe in God because of oysters. Theology professor and longtime friend Fisher Humphreys, speaking in my church, said, "Who but God would have thought of oysters?" He added, "One reason I know Heaven is going to be so interesting is that earth is so fascinating."

I believe in God because of worship. Once in a while–how I wish it were regularly–I will experience such an uplifting, soul-shattering moment of divine elation (I'm piling up words here because describing those moments is impossible) when my soul is yanked right out of my body. I have sat in the sanctuary of my church, the First Baptist Church of Jackson, Mississippi, and reveled in the experience of the great orchestra, the massive choir, and the uplifting sights and words of inspiration, all combined to pluck my heartstrings like a ukulele, and I wanted to cry. My soul yearned for more of this, and I knew it was just for a moment, perhaps 30 seconds at most, and then I would sink back into being myself. When that happens, I know something: There is more. We live in that which is partial, but one day, I shall see and know as I am seen and known. The partial shall be done away with. And I will join with the worshipers and singers and musicians of the ages and worship the way it was intended. Revelation 5 pictures just such a magical moment when this will happen. I can't wait.

O God, little children praise Thee perfectly. And so would we. And so would we.

I believe in God because of certain saints who have touched my life. I could tell you what saintly Marguerite Briscoe, Maude "Maugie" Sparks and my Grandma Bessie Lowery McKeever did for me, what they said, but you would not be impressed, and you would say that was not enough to make this list. But the fact is they didn't have to do anything. They just touched my life, and when they had passed, I knew I had been with God. I believe in God because of them.

I want someone to believe in God because they have known me.

I believe in God because He has spoken to me. At several critical points in my life when I needed direction, an inner voice directed me to a scripture that turned out to be so perfect and so right that I know it was God.

God found me as a 21-year-old college senior, singing in the church choir and He said, "I want you in the ministry." Six years later, while I was on my knees praying in a San Antonio hotel, He told me I was not to teach history in college (while pastoring on the side, as had been my intent) but I was to pastor churches. He spoke to me about marrying Margaret Henderson when I was 22, spoke to me about not going to certain churches and again about going to several over the years since, and spoke to me about retirement and a hundred other things. Jesus said, "My sheep hear my voice" (John 10:27).

I believe in God because of the incredible testimony of Scripture. Having devoted my adult life (and much of my youth) to reading and studying the Bible, I come now to my 80th year on this earthly sod to say I am far more impressed by the Scripture's existence, its miraculous contents, its stunning wisdom, its amazing applicability to every situation, its unity throughout, and a thousand other traits. God's Word is in a class by itself. I defy anyone to find a book written thousands of years ago that combines such diversity and yet is so unified, and that is so appropriate to our daily lives today.

This book is unique. Moses told the Israelites, "What great nation is there that has such statutes and righteous judgments as are in all this law which I set before you this day?" (Deuteronomy 4:8).

Indeed!

And John Ortberg's one big reason for believing in God?

Jesus believed.

There is no one else more worth trusting than Jesus.

This, Ortberg says, is the best reason for believing. "There is simply no other source—no book, no guru, no hunch, no personal experience—worth betting the farm on."

You and I are betting the farm on Jesus.

Ortberg's quotations are keepers. Elton Trueblood (Quaker theologian of a past generation; his books are wonderful; we used to have him at our annual Southern Baptist gatherings) said, "A Christian is a person who, with all the honesty of which he is capable, becomes convinced that the fact of Jesus Christ is the most trustworthy that he knows in his entire universe of discourse."

George MacDonald, who had such an influence on C. S. Lewis, said, "I can only say with my whole heart that I hope we have indeed a Father in heaven; but this man *says he knows.*"

John Ortberg speaks of Bill Moore, of whom he learned in one of Lee Strobel's books, *The Case for Faith*. Bill Moore grew up in poverty, lived as a criminal, and killed a man for five thousand dollars. He was sentenced to death and sent to death row in the prison. That's where some men from church found him and shared the gospel with him. Until that moment, Bill Moore had never heard the message of Jesus.

Moore turned his life over to Jesus and then began telling others about him. Eventually, he became known in the prison as "the peacemaker." Outsiders began sending people to him on death row for counseling. The man became such a strong believer, he even had an influence on the family of the man he killed. People began writing letters on his behalf. In time, his sentence was commuted and then he was paroled.

These days, says John Ortberg, Bill Moore heads a couple of ministries in housing projects. Strobel asked him, "Bill, what in the world turned your life around? Was it a new medication? Was it some kind of rehab program? Was it a new approach to counseling?"

Bill said, "No, Lee. It wasn't any of that stuff. It was Jesus Christ."

Ortberg concludes with this: "Atheism really has nothing to say to a guy on death row. Because when you're living on death row (and we're all living on death row), there's really only one thing you want to know."

Funny way to end a chapter. But there it is.

We're all living on death row.

Let me add something to Ortberg's one big reason to believe (and that being that "Jesus believed"). I love what the Lord said to Nicodemus in John chapter 3....

–If I told you earthly things (which you can verify) and you do not believe, how can you believe when I speak to you of Heavenly things? (John 3:12).

–No one has been to Heaven except the One who came from there, even the Son of Man. (John 3:13) The Lord Jesus is our Authority on Heaven, seeing as how He is a native of that far country.

–The Old Testament story of Moses putting a serpent on a pole and anyone who looked at it was healed is a picture of Me, said Jesus. "Even so must the Son of Man be lifted up, that whoever believes in Him should not perish but have eternal life" (Numbers 21 and John 3:14-15).

– "For God so loved the world that He gave His only begotten Son that whosoever believeth in Him should not perish but have everlasting life" (John 3:16).

If you know what people on death row are dying to learn, it would be a crime not to tell them, friend.

Jesus Christ. He is "the way, the truth, and the life" (John 14:6). And that's it.

There is no other person and no other way (Acts 4:12).

So, listen up. God is speaking.

CHAPTER THREE

God Has Spoken to Me. You Too?

How does God speak to us? Answer: Any way He pleases.

All possibilities are on the table.

Our Lord Jesus said we could expect to hear from Him. "My sheep hear my voice," He said. "I know them, and they follow Me" (John 10:3,16,27). It's standard procedure.

Henry Blackaby has famously said, "If you're not hearing from God on a regular basis, you're missing out on one of the most basic parts of the Christian life."

The greatest way God speaks to us is through His Word. Sometimes that comes from a passage while we are reading the Bible, and sometimes God speaks to us when no Bible is anywhere near.

God spoke to me when He called me in 1961, when He told me to marry Margaret in 1962, and when He said I was to pastor churches and not teach in college, in 1967. Those were fairly normal, I think. Here are my not-so-normal experiences of God invading me with His Word...

February 1975.

I was in my second year of leading the First Baptist Church of Columbus, Mississippi. I was 34 years old.

Racial tensions were high in the Deep South at that time. A number of our churches had split over the decision to open their membership to all races. I was determined we would do this in a Christ-honoring and unified way.

The Columbus church had a number of foreign students from African countries in worship services each Sunday, all enrolled at the local woman's university. But no person of color had ever become a member of our church. So, in February, when Kezia Chogo of Kenya indicated that "God is leading me to unite with this church," I began calling key leaders, asking them to get on their knees and begin praying. The time had come. We wanted to do this right.

I visited with Kezia on campus and gave her a book on our beliefs. "Read this and jot down your questions. Let me know when you finish."

I was stalling for time. To wait upon the Lord is not the work of an hour or a day.

A couple of weeks later, Kezia finished the book. We sat in the commons room in her dorm and talked about the procedure the following Sunday when she would join the church.

I wanted to prepare her for what might happen.

I said, "I'm going to have to ask if anyone is opposed to your joining the church. We don't normally do that. But if I don't, I'll never hear the last of it."

But I assured her, "The congregation will be delighted to welcome you, Kezia. Please know that."

"However, there is always the possibility that someone may say something unkind. I hope they won't, but they might. This does not mean they're not Christian, only that they have not grown in certain areas."

She assured me she was fine with all of that. We prayed, and I returned home.

For reasons long forgotten, my wife and our three children were away that afternoon. I was in the house alone. So, I devoted a couple of hours to praying and reading Scripture.

I was burdened, wanting to do this right, and concerned that the enemy not sabotage it.

I would read a few verses, then get on my knees and pray. Read some more, pray some more.

And that's how it happened.

One verse made me angry.

Those who fear the Lord will rejoice when they see you, for you waited on the Lord. (Psalm 119:74).

I read that and thought, "That's the dumbest thing I've ever read!"

Now, when have you ever read a Scripture that made you angry? I could not recall one. Why did this one infuriate me?

I had no answer.

However, a couple of minutes later, as I'm on my knees beside the chair praying, the Lord explained that verse to me.

Those who fear the Lord. That's the Lord's people, those who truly know Him.

They will rejoice when they see you. When you stand before them with your recommendation, they will gladly receive it.

Because you waited on the Lord. You did not run ahead of the Lord but waited for Him to do this in His way.

I cannot describe how good that felt. I knew it was a message from the Lord.

Sunday morning went well. I presented Kezia, the congregation enthusiastically welcomed her. Of the four people who voted against her as a member, one paid her college tuition the next semester. The congregation stood in line for 15 minutes to greet Kezia and welcome her. A lot of tears were shed that morning.

We had waited on the Lord and done it His way and He had the victory.

<u>Summer of 1989.</u>

I was in my third and final year of pastoring a church in North Carolina, the most difficult pastorate of my life. After arriving at that church, I learned that for over thirty years a small group had fought the two previous pastors. Soon after I moved in, in the summer of 1986, they started in on me. Then, in my third year, they began a campaign to fire me. The stress was enormous.

To deal with the relentless stress, Margaret and I began a pattern of long conversations and prayer out on the back porch. We would talk and cry, fuss and pray, but we agreed that once we went inside the house, we left it all out there.

One evening during our back-porch time, I was about to read the 67th Psalm. I have no memory of why that particular scripture. But as I began, everything inside me said, "No. Read Psalm 66."

I could not have told you what either one was about.

When I began reading, we saw the Lord was sending us a message.

In the middle of the 66th Psalm, we came upon this:

For You, O God, have tested us; You have refined us as silver is refined. You brought us into the net; You laid affliction on our backs. You caused men to ride over our heads. We went through fire and through water. But You brought us out into a place of abundance.

We were stunned. The passage was perfectly describing our experience in the hardest three years of our lives. We read it again and talked about it.

And then, Margaret--always more sensitive spiritually than I--did something.

As we began praying, thanking Him for this Scripture, Margaret said, "And Lord, You are promising to lead us out into a place of abundance. So, we're claiming that."

I had not read that as a promise, but once she said it, I saw that's exactly what it was. God was promising to lead us out of that situation which had been unbelievably difficult into a place of abundance.

Thereafter, as we prayed and put our trust in Him, we never failed to thank Him for promising to lead us into a place of abundance.

What was that place of abundance, we wondered?

We ended up taking a one-year paid leave from that church with plans to relocate as God led. During that twelve-month interim, I preached in a lot of places, I worked at writing a book, and we sold our house and moved into an apartment. We wanted to be ready when God called.

We moved to the New Orleans area in September of 1990 and I began pastoring the First Baptist Church of Kenner, across the street from the international airport. The church was in trouble, still struggling to recover from a massive split some 18 months earlier. It seemed that God's plan was that the wounded church and this bruised pastor would help one another to heal.

From time to time, Margaret and I would wonder out loud, "How is this the place of abundance which God promised us?" It felt like anything but that in many ways. The church was struggling to stay afloat, people were divided, and the city was difficult.

Sometimes my prayer would sound like this: "Is this your abundant place, Father? There is so much sin in New Orleans. The church is divided, some members carrying loads of guilt for their past behavior, and others burdened down with anger from that split. Is this a place of abundance, Lord?"

I'm not sure what we had expected, but this surely was not it.

Then one day God answered with the words of Romans 5:20.

Where sin abounded, grace did much more abound.

That came with a shock.

Abundant sin, abundant grace.

The New Orleans area is notorious for its abundant sin where--in certain areas at least--anything goes.

But God's grace is every bit as abundant and more.

This was indeed His place of abundance for us. The longer we stayed, the more we saw and understood.

I remained as pastor of that church for almost 14 years, then became the leader for the 130 Southern Baptist churches in metro New Orleans. A year later when Hurricane Katrina flooded the city and destroyed hundreds of thousands of homes and half our churches, we knew why God had put us there. For the next four years, we worked with people from all over the nation to help rebuild the churches of New Orleans. In hundreds of ways, God poured out His abundant grace upon us.

April 2004

As I left the pastorate and began the transition to leading that association of churches, I began to feel uncertain. This would be a huge change. I had pastored churches for 42 years, preaching several times a week, shepherding the Lord's people. Now, I would not have a flock and a thousand things would be different.

Could I do this? Would I be able to make the change? Would the pastors accept my leadership?

In the middle of that angst, one day I was in the car headed for the interstate. Suddenly, the Lord spoke to my heart with a verse of Scripture. I had to look it up to see where it was found.

Faithful is He who called you and He will bring it to pass.

First Thessalonians 5:24.

The Lord was assuring me, "I have called you to this work and I'll see to it."

I was not on my own. The Lord was in charge.

The peace that flooded my soul was overwhelming. God did some wonderful things through those five years of leading our churches and pastors.

Much of that involved recovery from Hurricane Katrina. And that's when He spoke to me again.

September 2005

Hurricane Katrina hit the Gulf Coast of Alabama, Mississippi, and Louisiana at the end of August 2005. Our area--metro New Orleans--had a lot of typical hurricane damage, but nothing like Mississippi, which lost entire cities along the coast. Mostly, what we had was flooding. Much of New Orleans is near or below sea level, and the city is dependent on a system of levees and canals to protect the city from flooding. When the hurricane breached a few of those walls, the city went underwater and was fighting for its life.

Many thousands of people lost their homes and hundreds were drowned. New Orleans was changed forever.

The Baptist associational offices are on the shore of Lake Pontchartrain, near the University of New Orleans. This area experienced a great deal of flooding. It was weeks before we could get back into our offices to check on things. Because our offices were elevated, we had very little damage, thankfully.

Finally, the water receded to the point that I could drive to the office, even though there was no electricity in the city.

It was an unforgettable drive of ten miles.

I'll never forget it. I was driving north on Elysian Fields Boulevard, surrounded by deadness on every side. Not another vehicle could be seen anywhere, other than the ruined ones lying where the floodwaters had found them. No human could be seen. The houses were vacant and ruined. The grass was brown and most of the trees had been killed by toxins in the floodwaters. The stores and homes were ruined. There was not a bird anywhere.

I was in tears.

"Lord," I said out loud, "it's not just that Walgreen's. Or that Wendy's. It's not just that house there and this one over here. It's all of them. It's the whole thing, Lord. And I don't know what to do about them."

Then, just that clearly, God spoke to my heart.

This is not about you. This is about Me.

Which, of course, was the point of I Thessalonians 5:24 in the first place.

God has this.

As He did. In time, someone else will write the history of all God did in those months and years following the greatest natural disaster to hit our part of the world ever. And, if I'm any judge, the story will come down to this: God was on the job; God was faithful.

He is so good.

I am beyond thankful for God's abundant grace and His infinite love.

Is God still speaking today?

Of course He is. He speaks through the "still small voice" of the Holy Spirit within the hearts of believers. He speaks through His Word, the Holy Scriptures. He speaks to us through other people and by circumstances. And once in a while, He sends us a verse or two of Scripture that is so perfect for our situation, we know this is from Him.

Psalm 66 is still on the job, still speaking...

Over the years, I have often returned to the Scripture which the Lord gave us in 1989 to remember, to read the entire chapter, and to reflect on its meaning. That's how I noticed something we had missed.

After the passage that speaks of men riding over our heads, God bringing us through the waters, etc., it speaks of the vows we made to Him.

I will go into Your house with burnt offerings; I will pay You my vows, which my lips have uttered, and my mouth has spoken when I was in trouble...

Why had I not noticed this before?

What vows did we make?

We had made no vows at the time.

So, that day we began praying and talking about the vows we should make to show our appreciation.

We came up with three vows to show our appreciation to the Father for His graciousness to us. We would:

--a) live simply

--b) give generously

--c) encourage other pastors

Those three vows have been our guides ever since, and remain to this day, some thirty years later.

The 66th Psalm ends with this praise:

Blessed be God, who has not turned away my prayer, nor His mercy from me.

Indeed!

CHAPTER FOUR

The Book That Understands Us!

His name was Emile Cailliet. In later life he became a professor at the University of Pennsylvania and then Princeton Theological Seminary. How he came to faith in Christ is an amazing testimony to the work of the Holy Spirit and the uniqueness of the Holy Scriptures.

Cailliet was born in a small French town, received an education that "was naturalistic to the core," and grew up a pagan. He did not lay eyes on a Bible until he was 23 years old. As a lad of 20, he fought on the front lines of World War I and saw atrocities unspeakable. If he had been an atheist before the horrors of that war, his unbelief was now set in stone.

When a German bullet felled Cailliet, an American field ambulance crew saved his life. In time, his badly shattered arm was fully restored during a 9-month hospital stay. While recovering, he married a Scotch-Irish lass he had met in Germany just before the war. She was a deeply committed Christian. Cailliet later said, "I am ashamed to confess that she must have been hurt to the very core of her being as I made it clear that religion would be taboo in our home."

Emile informed his wife that no Bible would ever be allowed in their home. And yet, he found himself longing for meaning in life.

In his reading — and Emile Cailliet was a voracious reader — he went through everything he could find to satisfy the yearnings of his heart and soul. He said, "I had been longing for a book that would understand me."

A book that would understand me.

Unable to find such, Cailliet decided to prepare one of his own. Over the next decade, he filled a leather-bound pocketbook with significant quotations gleaned from his reading. He said, "The quotations, which I numbered in red ink for easier reference, would lead me as it were from fear and anguish, through a variety of intervening stages, to supreme utterances of release and jubilation."

At least, that was the plan.

Finally, the day arrived when Emile Cailliet put the finishing touches on his masterpiece, a book that would understand him. He walked outside the house, sat down under a tree, looked around at the bright blue sky, and opened his precious anthology. This was going to be a great experience.

"As I went on reading, however, a growing disappointment came over me."

Far from speaking to his life and situation, the various quotations simply reminded Cailliet of their context, of where he had found them, and nothing more.

"I knew then that the whole undertaking would not work, simply because it was of my own making." Dejected, he put the book back in his pocket.

He had no idea what to do then.

But God did.

God was up to something at that exact moment.

Cailliet later said, "At that very moment, my wife, who incidentally knew nothing of the project on which I had been working, appeared at the gate of the garden, pushing the baby carriage."

It had been warm that afternoon and as she and the baby made their way toward the marketplace, they found the boulevard crowded. Since they had only recently arrived in that village, she did not know the name of the side street down which she now turned. Within moments the cobblestones were rattling the carriage so badly she knew she would have to turn aside. Just then, she spotted a patch of grass beyond a small arch and pulled onto it for a moment of rest.

The small grassy lot led to an outside stone staircase which she proceeded to climb without fully realizing what she was doing. At the top, she found a long room with the door wide open. She walked in.

At the far end sat a white-haired man working intently at a desk and not noticing her. As Madame Cailliet looked around, she saw a carved cross on the wall. That's when she became aware that she had entered a church, a French Huguenot church building hidden away ("as they all are," Emile said in relating this story, "even long after the danger of persecution has passed").

The old gentleman was the pastor.

Emile's wife now found herself doing something completely out of character. She walked up to the old man at the desk and said, "Have you a Bible in French?" Smiling, he handed her a copy. She took it and walked out without another word. Inside, her mind was flooded with blended joy and guilt.

At home, she began to apologize. She knew Emile had forbidden the Bible to be brought into their home and here she had gone out and asked for one. As she began her confession, Emile interrupted her.

"A Bible, you say? Where is it? Show me. I've never seen one before!"

Don't miss that. He had never seen the book he had banned from their home.

Emile says, "I literally grabbed the book and rushed to my study with it." He opened it at random and came upon the Beatitudes. "I read and read and read — now aloud with an indescribable warmth surging within… I could not find words to express my awe and wonder. And suddenly the realization dawned upon me: This was the Book that would understand me!"

He read deeply into the night, mostly the Gospels. And as he read, the One of whom they spoke, the One who spoke in them and was depicted in them came alive to Emile Cailliet.

"The providential circumstances amid which the Book had found me now made it clear that while it seemed absurd to speak of a book understanding a man, this could be said of the Bible because its pages were animated by the Presence of the Living God and the Power of His mighty acts. To this God I prayed that night, and the God who answered was the same God of whom it was spoken in the Book."

(Cailliet's story here is an excerpt from the July 1974 of Eternity Magazine, a wonderful publication that ended its ministry in 1988.)

Before leaving the subject, let me share one more quote.

You know the name of Charles Colson. After serving in the Nixon White House, and while spending time in prison for his part in the Watergate cover-up, he came to faith in Christ and later formed Prison Fellowship. Speaking on the specialness of God's Word, Colson admitted that at first, the historical reliability of the

Bible was of no concern to him. He changed his mind only when he began to see the power of Scripture in transforming the lives of prisoners.

"My convictions have come, not from studies in Ivory Tower academia, but from life in what may be termed the front-line trenches, behind prison walls where Christians grapple in hand-to-hand combat with the prince of darkness. In our prison fellowships, where the Bible is proclaimed as God's holy and inerrant revelation, believers grow, and discipleship deepens. Christians live their faith with power. Where the Bible is not so proclaimed, faith withers and dies. Christianity without biblical fidelity is merely another passing fad in an age of passing fads."

(Quoted in a sermon by Rod Benson on the www.forMinistry.com website of the American Bible Society.)

The Bible you hold in your hands is one remarkable book, the most amazing one ever.

Now, if you are running from God, you may not care for a "book that understands you." But if you are ready to stop fighting and listen for a message from Heaven, this is the Book.

Shhhh. Listen. God is speaking.

CHAPTER FIVE

Perhaps the Last Thing You'd Expect to Find in Scripture

Germ warfare is in Holy Scripture. And that is a story in itself.

It would be easy for us modern sophisticates to say the Lord Jesus did not understand microscopic/scientific things like bacteria, viruses, and germ warfare. Louis Pasteur was still eighteen centuries in the future.

But we would be wrong. Bad wrong.

Our ignorance is abominable. His wisdom is unbounded.

If Jesus were Who He claimed to be, and the One Scripture declares Him to have been, He certainly knew the importance of cleanliness and purity for us humans.

It's little things like this that trip up some moderns. Reading the Bible, they get hung up on terms like "the four corners of the world," "the sun rising," and heaven being "up there somewhere"–all colloquialisms which we understand and use every day, but which cause problems for those looking for some reason--any reason!--to reject the Holy Word.

But that's not the entire story.

You want to see germ warfare in Scripture? It's there. In the Old Testament, where God gave the Law to Israel through Moses, He made provisions for their health. All they had to do was to obey Him.

I've got a great story on this, one that formed a critical foundation block in my spiritual life at a time when I needed it.

But first, let's mention see the texts in question.

Texts in which God protects His people from disease

– "And he placed the laver between the tent of meeting and the altar and put water in it for washing. And from it Moses and Aaron and his sons washed their hands and their feet. When they entered the tent of meeting, and when they approached the altar, they washed, just as the Lord had commanded Moses" (Exodus 40:30-32).

–The bodies of sacrificial beasts were often burned "outside the camp." See Leviticus 4:12,21, and 8:17 for starters. (Also, in reference to that, see Hebrews 13:10-14.)

–Leviticus 11 lists foods which were unclean (and thus forbidden) to God's people. We know now that those animals were most susceptible to disease and thus food from them would pose the biggest threat to Israel.

–Leviticus 12 has laws for the purification of the mother after childbirth. Blood issues were a major concern, and for good reason.

–Leviticus 13 gives tests for leprosy and provisions for quarantining those with communicable diseases. Some consisted of a mere seven days, but in the case of all-out leprosy, "all the days during which he has the infection; he is unclean. He shall live alone; his dwelling shall be outside the camp" (13:46). In his amazing book, *None of These Diseases*, S. I. McMillen says it was the discovery of the quarantine from Scripture that stopped the Black Plague in its tracks.

–Leviticus 14-15 contain provisions for cleansing unhealthy places. It might involve tearing down a house altogether, burning one's contaminated clothing, or simply a time of waiting.

– "And the Lord will remove from you all sickness, and He will not put on you any of the harmful diseases of Egypt which you have known..." (Deuteronomy 7:15). This is a restatement of Exodus 15:26. *If you will give earnest heed to the voice of the Lord your God, and do what is right in His sight, and give ear to His commandments, and keep all His statutes, I will put none of the diseases on you which I have put on the Egyptians; for I, the Lord, am your healer.*

—And this most practical text: "You shall also have a place outside the camp and go out there, and you shall have a spade among your tools, and it shall be when you sit down outside, you shall dig with it and shall turn to cover up your excrement" (Deuteronomy 23:12-13).

God even provided for the sanitary disposal of human sewage! What a practical Lord!

Okay. Now for the story I promised....

How I came to question God....and got an answer that stunned me!

During college I was reading Sinclair Lewis' *Elmer Gantry*, his prize-winning novel of a renegade preacher who would be played by Burt Lancaster on the big screen. In the story, two preachers are chatting. One is leaving the ministry. He is tired of making excuses and alibis for God, he says. "All those contradictions in the Bible. I know we can come up with arguments and explanations for them, but I'm tired of it."

Then he said, "And another thing. If Jesus was Who He claimed to be, instead of doing all those healing miracles, which had such a temporary effect, why didn't He do something of lasting benefit to mankind.... like give us a sanitation code?" (These are not exact quotes.)

I read that and was stopped short. Great question, I thought. Wonder why the Lord didn't? I had no answer. Nor did Sinclair Lewis propose one.

Amazing how egotistical doubt can be. You come up with a question for which you are convinced there is no answer. So, convinced there is no answer, you don't look for one.

And, I suspect that, even if you are a believer, you walk around with this spiritual parasite sucking the life out of you, this unacknowledged doubt sapping your strength and joy in the Lord.

I was a believer, called to the ministry, and preparing to head to seminary. But here I was harboring a nagging doubt that was troubling me.

I went forward, believing that this could be a serious weakness in the Scripture story, but not knowing what to do about it. Not wanting this to be the end of the story.

But then, when I had suffered enough, God stepped in.

"But God." That two-word game-changer is found all through Scripture. (Genesis 8:1; 31:42; 50:20. I Samuel 23:14. I Kings 5:4. Nehemiah 9:17. Psalm 49:15; 73:26. Isaiah 40:8. Jonah 2:6. Matthew 19:26. John 1:18. Acts 2:24; 3:15; 5:39. Romans 5:8. I Corinthians 1:27. 2 Timothy 2:9.)

At some point in seminary, I came across S. I. McMillen's book, *None of These Diseases*. It was like a lightning bolt to my fears and doubts, burning them to a crisp, leaving me forever changed.

McMillen tells the story of Dr. Ignaz Semmelweis, a maternity doctor in Europe in the early to mid-1800s. Concerned that too many women were dying after giving birth, he began studying procedures of his hospital. He noticed, among other things, that the medical staff went straight from performing autopsies in the morning to examining women patients in adjoining rooms, without so much as washing their hands.

For good reason, the mortality rate was horrendous.

On nothing more than a hunch Semmelweis put a basin of water in the examination room and required all doctors to wash their hands after the autopsies. They griped—doctors do not like change! —but the rate of infection and death dropped drastically. Semmelweis could not explain why washing worked, only that it did. But his staff kept protesting that this was contrary to accepted medical science of the time!

Then, after a particularly bad day in which 11 of 12 women in a ward died, Semmelweis put a basin of water at the foot of each bed. Doctors would be required to wash their hands after each examination. They did this reluctantly--the complaining was relentless–and the death rate dropped to almost nothing. However, the medical staff raised such a ruckus that Semmelweis was fired. They threw out the basins and went back to the old ways, and mothers went back to dying.

Semmelweis moved to another country, became head of another maternity hospital, and installed the same procedures. As before, the mortality rate dropped significantly, but once again the doctors made life so miserable for him, the man lost his mind. He died at age 47.

Today, a statue of Semmelweis beside a mother and baby stands at the University of Chicago Medical School.

In his book, Dr. McMillen points out that 1500 years before the birth of Christ, God had told Israel that after touching a dead body, they were to be unclean for a period of time, were to burn their clothing, and to wash themselves, but not in a basin of stagnant water. Scripture called for *running* water!

Some might insist, said McMillen, that Moses had learned all these things from growing up in Egypt. After all, Acts 7:22 says *Moses was learned in all the wisdom of the Egyptians.* McMillen dismisses this. The current practice in Egypt at that time called for dung to be applied to wounds and holes to be drilled in skulls to cure headaches!

Moses said he got this wisdom from God on Sinai. It was such a remarkable advance in medical science, that we should believe him.

Too bad Sinclair Lewis didn't know this. His ignorant slander likely caused many a person to stumble.

This account alone should bolster our confidence in the Scriptures as the very word of God.

Somewhere I read that in the late 1940s, a large group of college students was polled on religion and modern science. They voted overwhelmingly that God did not understand something so advanced as radar.

Radar? These days elementary school children understand radar.

Just so easily do people become overly impressed by their latest scientific discoveries and, in their pride at unveiling one more part of the wonderful mechanics of the vast universe, turn away from believing in an omniscient, all-present, ever-loving God.

Man, it seems, wants so badly to dismiss God that he will grab at anything available. The Lord said to Jeremiah, *My people have...forsaken Me, the fountain of living waters, and have hewed out for themselves cisterns, broken cisterns that can hold no water.* (Jeremiah 2:13)

Such is the determined foolishness of mankind.

We leave this subject with the triumphant benediction of Jude 24...

Now to Him who is able to keep you from stumbling, and to make you stand in the presence of His glory blameless with great joy, to the only God our Savior, through Jesus Christ our Lord, be glory, majesty, dominion and authority, before all time and now and forever. Amen.

CHAPTER SIX

"The Bible Says"--That may not be as simple as it sounds

In the Arizona desert, there is a little critter called a "stick lizard." On days when the temperature is out of sight and the desert floor sizzles like a hot plate, this little animal runs around with a stick in its mouth. When its feet become too hot to stand, it stops, pokes the stick in the sand, and climbs up on it. After they cool, he hops off, grabs the stick in his mouth, and he's gone again. — I want to be like the stick lizard: going on and doing my job when everyone else stays home because they can't take the heat.

I love that little story. I found it in Smithsonian Magazine some years back.

Well, I did, and I didn't.

It was actually a letter to the editor of the Smithsonian. But I never forgot it and have used the stick lizard in the occasional article, devotional and sermon over these years. He seems like such a survivor, a tiny creature that has figured a way to overcome obstacles.

And now, I find out that it may not exist.

A Facebook friend who pastors a church in Arkansas commented that according to "clay.thompson @arizonarepublic.com," the stick lizard does not exist.

It's "old-timer, tall-tale hooey," he said, but "it amuses the tourists."

Another great sermon illustration shot down by reality.

Now, in all fairness, all we have said is that an Arkansas pastor "said" someone named Clay Thompson says this. I have not followed up to see if there is such a person, if he said such, and if he has evidence the critter is fictional. The letter to the editor of the Smithsonian does not make the animal exist, and the report of a naysayer does not prove he doesn't.

Having a reference to cite as the source of a great story or quote is always good policy, but simply saying "Thom Dicken Hairy said this" does not make it so.

People play this little game with the Scriptures. Case in point.

A couple of years back, I ran across a newspaper column where prominent columnist Cal Thomas was taking a potshot at some preacher or other for living lavishly. To make his point he quoted our Lord: "Do not acquire gold or silver or copper for your money belts, or a bag for your journey, or even two tunics, or sandals, or a staff, for the worker is worthy of his support" (Matthew 10:9-10).

Did Jesus say that? He sure did. The quote is accurate.

But that's not all He said on that subject.

Sometime later, Jesus reversed those very instructions.

"'When I sent you out without purse and bag and sandals, you did not lack anything, did you?' And they said, 'No, nothing.' And He said unto them, 'But now, let him who has a purse take it along, likewise also a bag, and let him who has no sword sell his robe and buy one....'" (Luke 22:35-36).

So, to quote the first passage as authoritative for believers today without any reference to the second is either to reveal one's ignorance of the Word or to practice deceit.

How the practice of deceit and manipulation with quotes operates.

Once in a while, when you come across a great quotation, the author's name underneath will reveal him/her to be a novelist. When tracing the quote back to its source, we often discover that the author put those words in the mouth of one of his characters. So, in a way the author said those words, and, in another way, he didn't.

One way writers convey a controversial point without enraging readers is to have a character spout those words. Readers may get mad at the character but not at the writer.

People quote Shakespeare all the time, when what they should be doing (depending on the situation) is saying, "Shakespeare has King Lear saying" a thing.

One of our old-time hymns speaks of "such a worm as I." Where did that put-down of humans come from? Perhaps from Job 25:6: "How much less man, that maggot, and the son of man, that worm!"

But the speaker of those words was Bildad, one of Job's flawed counselors. God did not say this, even though "it's in the Bible." (The modern rendition of that hymn changed the line to "a sinner such as I.")

Quoting from the book of Job is always chancy, since it's almost entirely a conversation men are having with one another. Even the protagonist, Job himself, is not always on target with his words. (Job does however speak some great, great words of faith, such as 14:14; 19:25-26 and 23:12, three favorites of everyone.)

Serious truth-seekers and mature disciples of Jesus Christ will always want to be careful with their handling of the Word:

1) We must not take at face value any statement of "The Bible says....", no matter who says it. Manipulators count on the gullible being easily duped and never checking to see that their claims are authentic.

2) Like the Bereans of old (Acts 17:11), we will look up Scripture quotations to make sure they say what the speaker/writer claims and that the context supports the interpretation.

3) We will be conservative in how we use Scripture, making sure to cite references accurately and never carelessly nor deceptively.

4) When pastors and teachers we know and respect are found to be misquoting Scripture or misusing it in these ways, we will prayerfully and humbly call this to their attention. It's the loving thing to do. (But we will be careful not to nit-pick.)

5) This is not to say, however, that quoting only part of a text is wrong. Scripture writers often quoted other scriptures, but almost never word-for-word. (I suspect a lot of that is due to their going by memory as well as the near impossibility of looking up every reference in a scroll somewhere to make sure they had the line correct. And, Scriptures were not divided into chapters and verses back then.)

Take, for example, the passage of Exodus 34:6-7 where God reveals His glorious attributes. It's quoted all through the Old Testament (Numbers 14:18; Nehemiah 9:17; Psalms 86:15; 103:8; 145:8; Jonah 4:2; and Joel 2:13.), but never verbatim.

6) God's people must always handle the Word of the Lord carefully and reverentially. I was performing a

wedding with the priest in a local Catholic church. During the rehearsal, it was decided that a bridesmaid would read a portion of Scripture during the wedding. The question arose as to how to get the text to her in the middle of the ceremony. Someone suggested we photocopy those verses so she would not have to carry the Bible itself. The priest said, "I'll type it up for you. I have such a reverence for the Word that I never photocopy it." I blushed as I remembered all the times, I had laid the Bible across the copy machine and hit "print."

7) When citing Scripture or when reading someone else's references to the Word, we always do well to keep in mind certain questions, whether we ask them or not:

–Does the Bible actually say this? Is the quote authentic?

–Does the Bible say that only in an earlier version, but later scholarship has shown the meaning to be something entirely different? (The spurious ending of Mark 16 comes to mind.)

–Did it mean to say what is being claimed? Just because the words form a certain sentence does not automatically mean the intent was a verbatim reading. Often figures of speech ("the eye of a needle" and "I am the door") are metaphors not to be taken literally.

–Does the context support the interpretation?

–Does Scripture anywhere cancel (or fulfill or end) a promise or command you are citing? (See the Cal Thomas reference above.)

Evangelist Billy Graham had a practice which I recommend. Instead of peppering his sermons with "The Apostle Paul says"–since Paul said so much, preachers find themselves quoting him a lot–Mr. Graham would simply say, "Scripture says." We have good precedent for that, since the Apostle Peter refers to Paul's writings as "scripture" (Second Peter 3:16).

Pastors who obsessively feel they have to give the chapter and verse for every scripture they cite are needlessly burdening their hearers. Even the Bible does not go to great lengths to make sure every reference is there. I smile at Hebrews 4:4, "For He has thus said somewhere...." (and proceeds to quote two different Old Testament texts). In Hebrews 5:6, we read: "Just as He says also in another passage...."

The teacher and preacher of the Word does not need to slavishly belabor getting all the references and quotes exactly right in order to be faithful. Sometimes, in the middle of a lesson or sermon or even a conversation, we remember the gist of a text and cite it and go on. So long as we are faithful in our use and accurate in the context, the Lord blesses His Word in the hearts of all who hear.

"For whatever was written in earlier times was written for our instruction, that through

perseverance and the encouragement of the Scriptures we might have hope." (Romans 15:4)

I must have been eight or nine years old. Walking up the West Virginia mountain to school in the mornings, I would often talk to God silently.

On one occasion, I recall thinking, "I will not say 'amen' and end this prayer. That way, the line will be open to the Lord all day long and I can keep on talking to Him."

In time I would come to understand that just as we want the Lord to listen to us throughout the day, He wants the same from us. He is always speaking, but not everyone hears.

Walter Moore was a repairman on office machines. He told me that once he was in a bank office hard at work while people were coming and going and the noise level was high. When five o'clock came, everyone shut off their machines and left the office. "That's when I noticed for the first time," he said, "that they had music piped in. You couldn't hear it for the noise."

Only those who can sit quietly and wait before the Lord hear what He says.

Listen! God is speaking, friend.

CHAPTER SEVEN

Caution: The Pastor Is About to Tell Us the Greek Word!

I wonder about this.

In his sermon, the pastor says "Now, in the original Greek, this word means…."

I wonder if church members roll their eyes.

Or, he says, "The Hebrew word used here is..."

Do the church members grimace and just try to get through it?

I suspect church members are often turned off by this little display of one-upsmanship from the preacher. It feels to some like he's showing off, bragging that he knows the original languages. Whether he does or not.

Okay.

Now, if the minister studied the language for a few years, he should be capable of bringing in the finer insights of the Word from the Greek or Hebrew.

But he must not overdo it by trying too hard or expecting too much.

I fear I've done this in the past. Forgive me, members of the six churches I've served.

When a pastor says, "Now, the verb tense in the Greek is aorist, which indicates the action has already happened and is over with, so therefore…." you can bet people are looking at their watches, wondering how much more of this they have to endure.

With rare exceptions, church members simply do not care what tense the verb is in. They do not care that this is the only place in the New Testament where this word is used. They do not care for the finer points of the language study which the pastor mastered in Bible school or seminary.

The man in the pew is worrying about his teenage daughter and the friends she's been running with. The woman in the pew is worried about her husband who seems too involved with his job and too absent from the home. The seniors in the pews are thinking about health issues, about financial matters, and about the uncertain future. The teens are thinking about each other.

What they are not thinking about is what tense that Greek verb is in. In fact, it's a sign of the disconnect we pastors have with our congregations that we think they are interested.

Five people are. Ninety-five could not care less.

Having said that, I want to qualify it. Once in a while, a wonderful insight from the Greek is worth the trouble. (Read on.) Even then, at least half the congregation will take a mini-vacation and skip out on the language study. And that's all right.

Sometimes, an insight is so good, so amazing, it's worth the trouble to get the riches to a few of the sharper, more eager, members even if it bypasses the others.

Here is one such insight from the Greek, a favorite of mine....

In the same way the Spirit helps our weakness. For we do not know how to pray as we should. But the Spirit Himself intercedes for us with groanings too deep for words. –Romans 8:26.

In the Greek, the little word translated *helps* is a compound word made up of 17 letters. *synantilambanomai*.

Here is how the word breaks down…

–syn is the prefix for "together," or "with."
–anti means "in front of," or "against."
–lambanomai is a form of the Greek verb meaning "to lift."

Put them together and you get a wonderful picture of what the Holy Spirit does for the child of God who "does not know how to pray as he should."

He gets on the other side (anti) and together with us (syn) gets under the burden and helps us lift it.

Think of making up a bed by yourself. But what a difference when a friend stands on the other side to help.

Have you ever tried to pull a crosscut saw alone? But with a friend on the other end, the work gets done.

When praying, we are hampered by a great weakness: We do not know how to pray as we should. But the Holy Spirit picks up the slack. He gets on the other side of our prayer burden, and together with us, lifts it to the Throne of Grace.

If that's not an encouragement to pray, there is none.

You're not alone when you go to pray. You're not doing this alone. The Spirit is on the job, assisting you.

And that's the last Greek lesson you'll hear from me.

Until the next time.

CHAPTER EIGHT

A few word studies to bless the serious Bible student

What made me want to study Greek and Hebrew in seminary was a couple of faithful preachers during my college years who sometimes gave us the meaning of a word in their sermons. Not too much, of course. It's easy to overdo. And nothing very technical. The guy in the pew does not care a whit about the aorist tense or pluperfect whatever, or that Josephus used this in one way and Herodotus another.

Pastors should do this sparingly, even though when they do it wisely and well, a word study can enrich Bible study and inspire the hearers.

Here are a few from Paul's Letter to the Philippians…

"…so that you may approve the things that are excellent, in order to be sincere and blameless until the day of Christ" (Philippians 1:10).

The word "sincere" here is rich in meaning. Our English word comes from the Latin "sin" meaning "without" and "ceres" meaning "wax." Without wax. We're told this refers to the shoddy practice of some sculptors long ago. While working on a piece of art, the marble might develop a crack. Rather than discard the piece or try to repair it, the unscrupulous artist might fill it with wax. It looked great and fooled the buyer.... until the piece was being displayed next to a roaring fire. The heat melted the wax, and the fraud was discovered. We might say a truly sincere person is without wax and can take the heat.

We used to speak of certain people being "plastic." By that we meant a cheap imitation of the real thing. Same point.

The Greek word for "sincere" in this verse is *heilikrines*. *Heile* comes from *helios* (sun) and *krino* means tested or judged. So, the idea is "sun-tested." I can recall hearing in earlier times of someone buying a suit in a store with artificial lighting. Once he took the suit outside the store, he quickly saw the workmanship or quality, or material or color was not what he had in mind. So, a sincere person can stand the light. Light-tested.

Lawmakers speak of "sunshine laws" which are intended to put a stop to secret sessions of committees during which they plan their open meetings. Turn the light on. Our Lord said, "Men love darkness rather than light" for a very good reason: Their deeds are evil.

We are to be people of the light. "Children of the light" in I Thessalonians 5:5. Jesus said, "There is nothing covered that will not be revealed; nothing hidden that will not be known. What I tell you in the darkness, speak in the light" (Matthew 10:26-27).

> *"...standing firm in one spirit, with one mind striving together for the faith of the gospel...." (Philippians 1:27).*

The word "striving" is s*ynathleo*, found only here in the New Testament. (oops. I did it.) *Syn* = together and *athleo* = to be an athlete, to contend in games. Think of a team working together. Eleven men line up across the football field, take their positions, and then follow their quarterback, their field captain. That's a great picture for the Lord's people operating in unison and harmony. Each one plays a different position, and if he's not in his place or does not follow his leader, the enemy breaks through and nothing good happens.

Everyone strives together for the faith of the gospel.

As the D-Day planning team broke up their final meeting in 1944, historians tell us that General Eisenhower's final words were "Gentlemen, it's one team—or we lose." The armies of numerous Allied nations were represented in that room. Yet they had to work together if they would overcome the common enemy.

Speaking of unity...

> *"...make my joy complete by being of the same mind, maintaining the same love, united in spirit, intent on one purpose" (Philippians 2:2).*

United in spirit; intent on one purpose (NASB).

First, "united in spirit." The Greek *sympsychos*, literally means "together-souled." The idea is harmonious, united in spirit. Then, "intent on one purpose." Literally the Greek means "the one thing minding" or "thinking the one thing."

Think of the last college football game you attended. A hundred thousand people in the stands, divided by politics and religion and race. And yet, their hearts were beating in unison, their minds set on one purpose.

In Jesus Christ we are to be "together-souled" and "together-minded." There is no place in the Kingdom for the silly divisions and partisanships we often joke about in our denomination. "Where you have two Baptists, you have three opinions."

God is not amused. Jesus prayed that "they all may be one, that the world may believe that Thou hast sent Me" (John 17:21).

Much is at stake; unity is essential.

"So then, my beloved, just as you have always obeyed, not as in my presence only but now much more in my absence, work out your salvation with fear and trembling" (Philippians 2:12).

The verb *katergazesthe* means "to work on to the finish," or "carry on to the goal."

Am I an expert on Greek? My seminary professors would smile at the very idea. Among other aids, I rely heavily on "Word Meanings in the New Testament" by Ralph Earle, published by Baker Book House in 1987. You can find it used, and it would be a wonderful purchase. It's one volume and large print.

CHAPTER NINE

10 Scriptures That Keep Drawing Me Back Again and Again.

It's fine to have your favorite Scriptures. They will have ministered to your soul and lifted your spirits when you needed it most.

Here are ten passages that I dearly love...

One. Romans 8 is the mother lode of spiritual insight.

Romans 8:26. *"In the same way, the Spirit helps us in our weakness. For we do not know how to pray as we should. But the Spirit Himself intercedes for us..."*

Now, if the Apostle Paul did not know how to pray, it's a lead-pipe cinch that you and I don't!

But, we're not to despair.

The Holy Spirit picks up the slack and helps us. He is our intercessor. (I admit to having no idea how that happens, how the Spirit intercedes with the Father; and see no point in trying to figure it out.) And then– this is where it gets good–in verse 34 the Lord Jesus is our intercessor. He is "at the right hand of the Father making intercession for us."

I think this is unique in Scripture: Romans 8:26 and 8:34 depicting both the Son and the Spirit interceding for us.

If we thought imagining the Spirit interceding was difficult, try to picture both the Spirit and the Son doing it! And yet, that's what we have here.

However...

In case we are tempted to say, "two members of the Trinity are interceding for us, so the Heavenly Father is out-voted from the first," Romans 8:31 does not allow that. "God is for us!" Meaning God the Father.

The first 30 verses of Romans 8 braid together the three-pronged truth that the Father is for us, the Son is for us, and the Spirit is for us. Then, pulling it all together, verse 31 says since God is for us, it doesn't matter who or what is against us! Such a truth is too wonderful for words and furnishes meditating material for a month or more.

On top of all this, we have verse 32: "He who did not spare His own Son, but delivered Him up for us all, how shall He not with Him freely give us all things?"

Since God has given us the best Heaven has, is He now going to start withholding further blessings?

This is just a taste of the riches of this chapter. But it does not yield its treasures to those who do a quick scan and rush on to other things. We must read it slowly, numerous times over several days, and think about it. Meditation on the Word of God can be the most productive activity any of us will ever do.

Two. Psalm 103 is saturated with wonders.

After memorizing this psalm and preaching it for years, one day I noticed in my grandmother's Bible a note beside verse 17. "Papa's favorite verse." I was stunned. That's the great-grandfather whom I never knew, but who preached the Word in and around the turn of the 20th century, traveling on horseback, in a wagon, or on foot.

Psalm 103 is all about God's love. The psalmist stacks insight upon insight, accolade upon accolade. We are not allowed to say the Old Testament is about wrath or law and the New about grace. It's all grace, from beginning to the end. The psalmist quotes from God's self-revelation in Exodus 34:6-7, perhaps the most quoted Old Testament passage of all.

Verse 14 is great comfort to those of us who sin. (That would be all of us!) *He Himself knows our frame; He is mindful that we are but dust.*

He who created us knows we are made of humble stuff. He knows He got no bargain when He saved us. When we sin, the only one surprised is us. And yet, God loves us still, as He did from the first. That's why He built into the system a fail-safe way back into His presence when we sin. It's called the cross, pre-figured by every altar in the Old Testament.

Three measurements of God's love are given in Psalm 103:11-13, then reinforced and extended in verse 17.

Three. Matthew 10:16ff so perfectly describes the life (the expectations, the conditions, the requirements) of the Christian worker.

As a young pastor, I would preach this passage using the outline of wise up, speak up, stand up, and look up (with maybe another 'up' point or two in there which I've forgotten!). It's the charter of God's people on assignment for Him.

Look at what He promised as we go forth to serve Him:

—We should expect difficulty and opposition. "I send you forth like sheep among the wolves." He assumes we know what that means. In Acts 14:22, Paul and Barnabas told the new believers something similar.

—As we go, we are representing Him. Is there a greater honor? We are ambassadors for Christ (2 Cor 5:20).

—People will treat us the way they treated Him. It is enough for the disciple that he be like the master. (10:25) We cannot say He didn't warn us!

–He will use us, even in our weakest, darkest moments. "It is not you who speak, but it is the Spirit of your Father who speaks in you" (10:20). Acts 16 shows how God used Paul and Silas in jail. With their backs bleeding from the whipping they had received, and their feet locked into stocks, they sang hymns and prayed. In the middle of their pain, they were faithful. We read, "And the other prisoners were listening to them" (Acts 16:25). This is such encouragement for believers who suffer for Christ.

–We will not lose our reward. (10:42) The Lord pays His bills and honors His promises. Hebrews 6:10 says if God were to forget those who have labored long and hard for Him, it would be sin on His part.

When I encounter pastors who have been mistreated by church leaders, I encourage them to set up residence in Matthew 10:16ff. just before moving on to Luke 6:27ff. The Lord Jesus did everything He could to prepare us for this.

There will be no room for bitterness; we are given no license for anger. By being faithful during our mistreatment, we often shine forth more brilliantly than ever and bear a strong witness to the watching world.

Four. Luke 18 is a favorite "prayer chapter."

I particularly love how the chapter begins and ends. To open, Jesus "was giving them a parable to show that at all times they ought to pray and not to faint." (Lose heart and quit.) This was followed by two parables and other insights about prayer. Even though it may not be immediately obvious to all, this chapter is all about prayer.

Then, the chapter concludes with the story of the blind beggar of Jericho. When Bartimaeus learns that Jesus of Nazareth is arriving in the city, he begins to call on Him, the essence of prayer. He continues calling loudly when some try to quieten him. He perseveres, demonstrating his faith. Finally, when he is brought before Jesus, the Lord asks him to get specific. "What exactly do you want?"

Enough with the generalities, Bartimaeus. What are you praying for? Up to this point, Bartimaeus had been asking the Lord to "have mercy on me." That's a broad category and could have meant a better begging place, some nice clothes, a few dollars. True, the Lord knew what he needed (see Matthew 6:8), but the question was whether the man praying knew his own need.

"Lord," he said, "I want to receive my sight."

The Lord wants us to call on Him, to remain steadfast in praying in spite of discouragement, and to pray specifically.

Five. The entire Second Epistle to the Corinthians is a huge favorite.

There are so many riches in this epistle, I'll mention just two.

The Apostle Paul uses numerous metaphors to describe believers in Christ. We are a fragrance for Christ (2:15), living letters (3:3), earthen vessels containing precious treasure (4:7), our bodies are earthly tents (5:1), we are ambassadors for Christ (5:20), and we are the temple of the living God (6:16).

I particularly stand in awe of Paul's reverse resume' given in chapter 11. To establish the authenticity of his apostleship, instead of trotting out his degrees and accomplishments, Paul points to his scars. "Imprisonments, beaten time without number, often in danger of death. Five times I received from the Jews thirty-nine lashes. Three times I was beaten with rods, once I was stoned, three times I was shipwrecked...."

Imagine the reaction if a prospective pastor handed something similar to a search committee: "I was run off from three churches, nearly lynched in a business meeting, beaten up by a distraught church member...."

Six. The 20th chapter of Acts is Paul's valedictory message to the pastors of Ephesus.

Paul reminisces about his time in their city preaching the gospel of Jesus and informs them of the trial awaiting him in Jerusalem. Then, he reminds these servants of the Lord of their call. That's verse 28.

The passage gives three terms for pastors–elders, pastors (shepherds), overseers. We have a high Christology here–in dying on the cross, Jesus shed the very blood of God.

Pastors, we learn, are appointed by the Holy Spirit to be overseers of the church.

The priority of the shepherd is made clear here: he is to be on guard for himself first (his health, his spirituality, his family) and for the flock second. Pastors who put care of the flock ahead of their own health, relationship to Christ, and concern for their family often end up losing all of it.

The flight attendant tells passengers, "In the event of a loss of cabin pressure, the air masks will drop out of the ceiling. If you are traveling with a child or handicapped person, secure your own mask first." Take care of yourself so you can help others.

Verse 28 is followed by a warning of two problems the church will face: 'savage wolves' from outside and 'perverse' people from inside. "Therefore, be on the alert." To our dismay, God's people keep getting blindsided by the group from inside the church. I hear them say, "But these were good people. How could they do such a thing?" Answer: Read your Bible. Be prepared for anything.

Since Paul will not see these beloved friends again, their visit ends with this: "He knelt down and prayed with them all. And they began to weep aloud and embraced Paul, and repeatedly kissed him, grieving especially over the word which he had spoken, that they should see his face no more." So emotional, so tender. Oh, that every minister were so well-loved.

Seven. In John 3, the Lord's discourse with Nicodemus, the verses most people rush past to get to verse 16 have special meaning to us.

Before the grand John 3:16, Jesus establishes His credentials. That's critical, because before making such a sweeping claim as this gospel-in-a-sentence, it's important to know how He is able to do so. What is His authority?

–verse 11. Jesus says, "I know what I'm talking about. I'm telling you what I have seen."

–verse 12. "But," He says, "If you don't believe when I tell you earthly things–which are verifiable, observable–how can you believe when I speak to you of heaven?" That question pops the balloons of those who say Scripture is reliable only in spiritual matters, but cannot be trusted regarding science, history, etc. We are not given the option to pick and choose.

–verse 13. "No one has been to Heaven except the One who came from there, Myself." Jesus says, "I am a native of Heaven. You can believe me when I talk about my home country." After all, who should know more about a country than a native. All others pontificating on heaven have just read the brochures; but Jesus knows!

–verse 14. Then, Jesus points to the cross. He does this by pulling out the single most obscure story in the Old Testament, the "snake on a pole," and shows how it points to the cross. The little incident takes up only four verses in Scripture (Numbers 21:6-9). Interestingly, not one word of commentary or explanation is given after the incident in Numbers.

The first indication the story had any spiritual value whatsoever came many hundreds of years later when Jesus spoke these words. That snake was the symbol of their sin. We are told, "He who knew no sin became sin for us…" (2 Corinthians 5:21).

And one thing more. All the Israelis had to do was look at the snake and they would live. Is that grace or what? No works whatsoever. The great 19th century British Pastor Charles Haddon Spurgeon came to Christ when he heard a layman preach on Isaiah 45:22, "Look unto me and be saved, all ye ends of the earth." Amen! Many an old-time preacher brought sermons on the theme "Look and live!"

Eight. We revel in I John 3:1ff.

What manner of love the Father has bestowed on us, that we should be called the children of God! And such we are.

For this reason, the world does not know us, because it did not know Him.

Beloved, now we are children of God, and it does not yet appear what we shall be. But we know that when He appears, we shall be like Him, for we shall see Him as He is. (That's reminiscent of Psalm 17:15.)

And everyone who has this hope in Him keeps himself pure, even as He is pure.

Nothing profound about my love of I John 3:1 and following. It's just wonderful in every way.

Nine. Ephesians 4-5 on the subject of unity in the Body of Christ.

Chapter 4 describes and defines the unity. And chapter 5 gives the means to it, specifically verse 21. "Be subject to one another in the fear of Christ."

I have long suspected that our people place small value on unity. Some almost seem to glory in their varied opinions and divided votes. I've known deacons who would insist on their right to oppose the recommendation of their leadership on the floor of the church because "I'm an American." Such thinking is shallow and contributes to the troubles of those churches.

"Is Christ divided?" asked Paul (I Corinthians 1:13). In Ephesians 4:3, leaders are told to be "diligent to preserve the unity of the Spirit in the bond of peace."

Why unity? Because the reputation of the Lord depends on it, the work of Christ is more efficient with it, the enemy is defeated by it, and fewer Christians are injured by the harshness of fellow believers in a unified church.

And where does unity come from? From loving believers submitting to Christ, their Head, and to each other. That's throughout Ephesians 5.

Submission to Jesus is easy but submitting to one another (5:21) is another story altogether. "Why should I submit when I'm in the right?" asks someone. Answer: So, when would you submit, when you're in the wrong? That's not submitting, but simply admitting you were wrong. To submit has to mean one thinks his position is the correct one, otherwise it's a meaningless concept.

Two motorists met on a one-lane bridge. The first guy leans out and yells, "I never back up for fools!" The second throws his car into reverse and says, "I always do."

Only the strong can submit and yield. The weak are unable to do something requiring such strength and self-control.

In I Corinthians 6:7, Paul asks a divided congregation, "Why not rather be wronged?" My opinion is that only the spiritual mature can handle such a concept. God help His church to be led by the mature.

Ten. I Thessalonians 4:14 brings tears to my eyes every time.

"For if we believe that Jesus died and rose again, even so God will bring with Him those who have fallen asleep in Jesus."

I have loved ones–beloved family members who mean everything to me–who are with the Lord. I miss them every day. My heart aches with their absence. In the words of Psalm 27:13, "I would have despaired had I not believed I would see the goodness of the Lord in the land of the living." But we have His word that we will see them again. Thank God for His promises. Thank God for the Lord Jesus Christ, our risen and living and returning Savior!

That's my list. I've worked on this lengthy article for many days. And in that time, have thought of a dozen other scriptures which mean everything to me, and which cry out to be included on this top-ten list. But, let's send it forth for the time being in hopes that it will encourage pastors to share with their people the texts which mean the most to them.

CHAPTER TEN

A Final Story About God's Amazing Word

In the days of Communist Russia, when Christians were an oppressed minority, those who risked their lives for Jesus and the gospel often found God at work in amazing ways.

This is one of those stories. No one who believes in the living God will be surprised; all who believe in Him will be blessed.

Missionary Ralph Bethea, Jr. was part of a team giving out Bibles in Russia. He went to one home where an old gentleman spoke of abandoning Communism and returning to the faith of his mother. He had no Bible, so Ralph gave him one.

The old gentleman clutched it to his chest, then invited in his neighbors and read it to them for four hours.

One man in the audience was a former KGB agent. As they talked, Ralph led him to faith in Christ.

When Ralph ran out of Bibles and many people were disappointed, the ex-KGB man said, "I know where there are 40,000 Bibles."

That government agency had confiscated them over the years, he explained.

Ralph Bethea and the man went to the agency and requested that they auction off all those Bibles. The Christian group ended up getting them for one thousand dollars.

At the warehouse where they had been stored, they took one of the boxes and cut it open. Ralph reached in and pulled out the first Bible. In appreciation and to honor his faithfulness, he handed it to the old man whom he had recently led to Christ.

The man opened it, stared at it, and began crying.

This was his mother's Bible–confiscated by the secret police 30 years earlier.

A God thing.

What a wonderful Lord we have.

How gracious of Him to give us His Word.

How thankful we should be for those who paid the ultimate price that we have possess a copy in our own language.

How faithful we should be in reading it, in sitting before our Lord with open Bible and waiting heart, to hear from Him.

Listen up, child of God. God is speaking.

www.ingramcontent.com/pod-product-compliance
Lightning Source LLC
Chambersburg PA
CBHW052204110526
44591CB00012B/2071